Book 1

C Programming Success in a Day

BY SAM KEY

&

Book 2

MYSQL Programming Professional Made Easy

BY SAM KEY

Book 1

C Programming Success in a Day

BY SAM KEY

Beginners' Guide To Fast, Easy And Efficient Learning Of C Programming

Programming #10: C Programming Success in a Day & MYSQL Programming Professional Made Easy

Programming #10: C Programming Success in a Day & MYSQL Programming Professional Made Easy

Table of Contents

Introduction

I want to thank you and congratulate you for purchasing the book, "C Programming Success in a Day – Beginners guide to fast, easy and efficient learning of Cc programming".

C. is one of the most popular and most used programming languages back then and today. Many expert developers have started with learning C in order to become knowledgeable in computer programming. In some grade schools and high schools, C programming is included on their curriculum.

If you are having doubts learning the language, do not. C is actually easy to learn. Compared to C++, C is much simpler and offer little. You do not need spend years to become a master of this language.

This book will tackle the basics when it comes to C. It will cover the basic functions you need in order to create programs that can produce output and accept input. Also, in the later chapters, you will learn how to make your program capable of simple thinking. And lastly, the last chapters will deal with teaching you how to create efficient programs with the help of loops.

Anyway, before you start programming using C, you need to get some things ready. First, you will need a compiler. A compiler is a program that will translate, compile, or convert your lines of code as an executable file. It means that, you will need a compiler for you to be able to run the program you have developed.

In case you are using this book as a supplementary source of information and you are taking a course of C, you might already have a compiler given to you by your instructor. If you are not, you can get one of the compilers that are available on the internet from MinGW.org.

You will also need a text editor. One of the best text editors you can use is Notepad++. It is free and can be downloadable from the internet. Also, it works well with MinGW's compiler.

In case you do not have time to configure or install those programs, you can go and get Microsoft's Visual C++ program. It contains all the things you need in order to practice developing programs using C or C++.

The content of this book was simplified in order for you to comprehend the ideas and practices in developing programs in C easily. Thanks again for purchasing this book. I hope you enjoy it!

Chapter 1: Hello World – the Basics

When coding a C program, you must start your code with the function 'main'. By the way, a function is a collection of action that aims to achieve one or more goals. For example, a vegetable peeler has one function, which is to remove a skin of a vegetable. The peeler is composed of parts (such as the blade and handle) that will aid you to perform its function. A C function is also composed of such components and they are the lines of codes within it.

Also, take note that in order to make your coding life easier, you will need to include some prebuilt headers or functions from your compiler.

To give you an idea on what C code looks like, check the sample below:

```
#include <stdio.h>

int main()

{

        printf( "Hello World!\n" );

        getchar();

        return 0;

}
```

As you can see in the first line, the code used the #include directive to include the stdio.h in the program. In this case, the stdio.h will provide you with access to functions such as printf and getchar.

Main Declaration

After that, the second line contains int main(). This line tells the compiler that there exist a function named main. The int in the line indicates that the function main will return an integer or number.

Curly Braces

The next line contains a curly brace. In C programming, curly braces indicate the start and end of a code block or a function. A code block is a series of codes joined together in a series. When a function is called by the program, all the line of codes inside it will be executed.

Printf()

The printf function, which follows the opening curly brace is the first line of code in your main function or code block. Like the function main, the printf also have a code block within it, which is already created and included since you included <stdio.h> in your program. The function of printf is to print text into your program's display window.

Beside printf is the value or text that you want to print. It should be enclosed in parentheses to abide standard practice. The value that the code want to print is Hello World!. To make sure that printf to recognize that you want to print a string and display the text properly, it should be enclosed inside double quotation marks.

By the way, in programming, a single character is called a character while a sequence of characters is called a string.

Escape Sequence

You might have noticed that the sentence is followed by a \n. In C, \n means new line. Since your program will have problems if you put a new line or press enter on the value of the printf, it is best to use its text equivalent or the escape sequence of the new line.

By the way, the most common escape sequences used in C are:

\t = tab

\f = new page

\r = carriage return

\b = backspace

\v = vertical tab

Semicolons

After the last parenthesis, a semicolon follows. And if you look closer, almost every line of code ends with it. The reasoning behind that is that the semicolon acts as an indicator that it is the end of the line of code or command. Without it, the compiler will think that the following lines are included in the printf function. And if that happens, you will get a syntax error.

Getchar()

Next is the getchar() function. Its purpose is to receive user input from the keyboard. Many programmers use it as a method on pausing a program and letting the program wait for the user to interact with it before it executes the next line of code. To make the program move through after the getchar() function, the user must press the enter key.

In the example, if you compile or run it without getchar(), the program will open the display or the console, display the text, and then immediately close. Without the break provided by the getchar() function, the computer will execute those commands instantaneously. And the program will open and close so fast that you will not be able to even see the Hello World text in the display.

Return Statement

The last line of code in the function is return 0. The return statement is essential in function blocks. When the program reaches this part, the return statement will tell the program its value. Returning the 0 value will make the program interpret that the function or code block that was executed successfully.

And at the last line of the example is the closing curly brace. It signifies that the program has reached the end of the function.

It was not that not hard, was it? With that example alone, you can create simple programs that can display text. Play around with it a bit and familiarize yourself with C's basic syntax.

Chapter 2: Basic Input Output

After experimenting with what you learned in the previous chapter, you might have realized that it was not enough. It was boring. And just displaying what you typed in your program is a bit useless.

This time, this chapter will teach you how to create a program that can interact with the user. Check this code example:

```
#include <stdio.h>

int main()

{

	int number_container;

	printf( "Enter any number you want! " );

	scanf( "%d", &number_container );

	printf( "The number you entered is %d", number_container );

	getchar();

	return 0;

}
```

Variables

You might have noticed the int number_container part in the first line of the code block. int number_container is an example of variable declaration. To declare a variable in C, you must indicate the variable type first, and then the name of the variable name.

In the example, int was indicated as the variable or data type, which means the variable is an integer. There are other variable types in C such as float for floating-point numbers, char for characters, etc. Alternatively, the name number_container was indicated as the variable's name or identifier.

Variables are used to hold values throughout the program and code blocks. The programmer can let them assign a value to it and retrieve its value when it is needed.

For example:

```
int number_container;

number_container = 3;

printf ( "The variables value is %d", number_container );
```

In that example, the first line declared that the program should create an integer variable named number_container. The second line assigned a value to the variable. And the third line makes the program print the text together with the value of the variable. When executed, the program will display:

```
The variables value is 3
```

You might have noticed the %d on the printf line on the example. The %d part indicates that the next value that will be printed will be an integer. Also, the quotation on the printf ended after %d. Why is that?

In order to print the value of a variable, it must be indicated with the double quotes. If you place double quotes on the variables name, the compiler will treat it as a literal string. If you do this:

```
int number_container;
```

```
number_container = 3;

printf ( "The variables value is number_container" );
```

The program will display:

```
The variables value is number_container
```

By the way, you can also use %i as a replacement for %d.

Assigning a value to a variable is simple. Just like in the previous example, just indicate the name of variable, follow it with an equal sign, and declare its value.

When creating variables, you must make sure that each variable will have unique names. Also, the variables should never have the same name as functions. In addition, you can declare multiple variables in one line by using commas. Below is an example:

```
int first_variable, second_variable, third_variable;
```

Those three variables will be int type variables. And again, never forget to place a semicolon after your declaration.

When assigning a value or retrieving the value of a variable, make sure that you declare its existence first. If not, the compiler will return an error since it will try to access something that does not exist yet.

Scanf()

In the first example in this chapter, you might have noticed the scanf function. The scanf function is also included in the <stdio.h>. Its purpose is to retrieve text user input from the user.

After the program displays the 'Enter any number you want' text, it will proceed in retrieving a number from the user. The cursor will be appear after the text since the new line escape character was no included in the printf.

The cursor will just blink and wait for the user to enter any characters or numbers. To let the program get the number the user typed and let it proceed to the next line of code, he must press the Enter key. Once he does that, the program will display the text 'The number you entered is' and the value of the number the user inputted a while ago.

To make the scanf function work, you must indicate the data type it needs to receive and the location of the variable where the value that scanf will get will be stored. In the example:

```
scanf( "%d", &number_container );
```

The first part "%d" indicates that the scanf function must retrieve an integer. On the other hand, the next part indicates the location of the variable. You must have noticed the ampersand placed in front of the variable's name. The ampersand retrieves the location of the variable and tells it to the function.

Unlike the typical variable value assignment, scanf needs the location of the variable instead of its name alone. Due to that, without the ampersand, the function will not work.

Math or Arithmetic Operators

Aside from simply giving number variables with values by typing a number, you can assign values by using math operators. In C, you can add, subtract, multiply, and divide numbers and assign the result to variables directly. For example:

```
int sum;

sum = 1 + 2;
```

If you print the value of sum, it will return a 3, which is the result of the addition of 1 and 2. By the way, the + sign is for addition, - for subtraction, * for multiplication, and / for division.

With the things you have learned as of now, you can create a simple calculator program. Below is an example code:

```
#include <stdio.h>

int main()

{

        int first_addend, second_addend, sum;

        printf( "Enter the first addend! " );

        scanf( “%d”, &first_addend );

        printf( "\nEnter the second addend! " );

        scanf( “%d”, &second_addend );

        sum = first_addend + second_addend;

        printf( "The sum of the two numbers is %d”, sum );

        getchar();

        return 0;

}
```

Chapter 3: Conditional Statements

The calculator program seems nice, is it not? However, the previous example limits you on creating programs that only uses one operation, which is a bit disappointing. Well, in this chapter, you can improve that program with the help of if or conditional statements. And of course, learning this will improve your overall programming skills. This is the part where you will be able to make your program 'think'.

'If' statements can allow you to create branches in your code blocks. Using them allows you to let the program think and perform specific functions or actions depending on certain variables and situations. Below is an example:

```
#include <stdio.h>

int main()

{

    int some_number;

    printf( "Welcome to Guess the Magic Number program. \n" );

    printf( "Guess the magic number to win. \n" );

    printf( "Type the magic number and press Enter: " );

    scanf( "%d", &some_number );

    if ( some_number == 3 ) {

        printf( "You guessed the right number! " );

    }

    getchar();

    return 0;

}
```

In the example, the if statement checked if the value of the variable some_number is equal to number 3. In case the user entered the number 3 on the program, the comparison between the variable some_number and three will return TRUE since the value of some_number 3 is true. Since the value that the if statement received was TRUE, then it will process the code block below it. And the result will be:

You guessed the right number!

If the user input a number other than three, the comparison will return a FALSE value. If that happens, the program will skip the code block in the if statement and proceed to the next line of code after the if statement's code block.

By the way, remember that you need to use the curly braces to enclosed the functions that you want to happen in case your if statement returns TRUE. Also, when inserting if statement, you do not need to place a semicolon after the if statement or its code block's closing curly brace. However, you will still need to place semicolons on the functions inside the code blocks of your if statements.

TRUE and FALSE

The if statement will always return TRUE if the condition is satisfied. For example, the condition in the if statement is 10 > 2. Since 10 is greater than 2, then it is true. On the other hand, the if statement will always return FALSE if the condition is not satisfied. For example, the condition in the if statement is 5 < 5. Since 5 is not less than 5, then the statement will return a FALSE.

Note that if statements only return two results: TRUE and FALSE. In computer programming, the number equivalent to TRUE is any nonzero number. In some cases, it is only the number 1. On the other hand, the number equivalent of FALSE is zero.

Operators

Also, if statements use comparison, Boolean, or relational and logical operators. Some of those operators are:

== – equal to

!= – not equal to

> – greater than

< – less than

>= – greater than or equal to

<= – less than or equal to

Else Statement

There will be times that you would want your program to do something else in case your if statement return FALSE. And that is what the else statement is for. Check the example below:

```
#include <stdio.h>

int main()

{

	int some_number;

	printf( “Welcome to Guess the Magic Number program. \n” );

	printf( “Guess the magic number to win. \n” );

	printf( "Type the magic number and press Enter: " );

	scanf( “%d”, &some_number );

	if ( some_number == 3 ) {
```

```
            printf( "You guessed the right number! " );
        }
        else {
            printf( "Sorry. That is the wrong number" );
        }
        getchar();
        return 0;
}
```

If ever the if statement returns FALSE, the program will skip next to the else statement immediately. And since the if statement returns FALSE, it will immediately process the code block inside the else statement.

For example, if the number the user inputted on the program is 2, the if statement will return a FALSE. Due to that, the else statement will be processed, and the program will display:

```
Sorry. That is the wrong number
```

On the other hand, if the if statement returns TRUE, it will process the if statement's code block, but it will bypass all the succeeding else statements below it.

Else If

If you want more conditional checks on your program, you will need to take advantage of else if. Else if is a combination of the if and else statement. It will act like an else statement, but instead of letting the program execute the code block below it, it will perform another check as if it was an if statement. Below is an example:

```
#include <stdio.h>

int main()

{

    int some_number;

    printf( “Welcome to Guess the Magic Number program. \n” );

    printf( “Guess the magic number to win. \n” );

    printf( "Type the magic number and press Enter: " );

    scanf( “%d”, &some_number );

    if ( some_number == 3 ) {

        printf( "You guessed the right number! " );

    }

    else if ( some_number > 3 ){

        printf( "Your guess is too high!" );

    }

    else {

        printf( "Your guess is too low!" );

    }

    getchar();

    return 0;

}
```

In case the if statement returns FALSE, the program will evaluate the else if statement. If it returns TRUE, it will execute its code block and ignore the following else statements. However, if it is FALSE, it will proceed on the last else statement, and execute its code block. And just like before, if the first if statement returns true, it will disregard the following else and else if statements.

In the example, if the user inputs 3, he will get the You guessed the right number message. If the user inputs 4 or higher, he will get the Your guess is too high message. And if he inputs any other number, he will get a Your guess is too low message since any number aside from 3 and 4 or higher is automatically lower than 3.

With the knowledge you have now, you can upgrade the example calculator program to handle different operations. Look at the example and study it:

```
#include <stdio.h>

int main()

{

        int first_number, second_number, result, operation;

        printf( "Enter the first number: " );

        scanf( “%d”, &first_number );

        printf( "\nEnter the second number: " );

        scanf( “%d”, &second_number );

        printf ( “What operation would you like to use? \n” );

        printf ( “Enter 1 for addition. \n” );

        printf ( “Enter 2 for subtraction. \n” );

        printf ( “Enter 3 for multiplication. \n” );

        printf ( “Enter 4 for division. \n” );
```

```
    scanf( “%d”, &operation );
    if ( operation == 1 ) {
        result = first_number + second_number;
        printf( "The sum is %d”, result );
    }
    else if ( operation == 2 ){
        result = first_number - second_number;
        printf( "The difference is %d”, result );
    }
    else if ( operation == 3 ){
        result = first_number * second_number;
        printf( "The product is %d”, result );
    }
    else if ( operation == 4 ){
        result = first_number / second_number;
        printf( "The quotient is %d”, result );
    }
    else {
        printf( "You have entered an invalid choice." );
    }
    getchar();
    return 0;
}
```

Chapter 4: Looping in C

The calculator's code is getting better, right? As of now, it is possible that you are thinking about the programs that you could create with the usage of the conditional statements.

However, as you might have noticed in the calculator program, it seems kind of painstaking to use. You get to only choose one operation every time you run the program. When the calculation ends, the program closes. And that can be very annoying and unproductive.

To solve that, you must create loops in the program. Loops are designed to let the program execute some of the functions inside its code blocks. It effectively eliminates the need to write some same line of codes. It saves the time of the programmer and it makes the program run more efficiently.

There are four different ways in creating a loop in C. In this chapter, two of the only used and simplest loop method will be discussed. To grasp the concept of looping faster, check the example below:

```
#include <stdio.h>

int main()

{

        int some_number;

        int guess_result;

        guess_result = 0;


        printf( "Welcome to Guess the Magic Number program. \n" );

        printf( "Guess the magic number to win. \n" );

        printf( "You have unlimited chances to guess the number. \n" );
```

```
    while ( guess_result == 0 ) {

        printf( "Guess the magic number: " );
        scanf( "%d", &some_number );
        if ( some_number == 3 ) {
            printf( "You guessed the right number! \n" );
            guess_result = 1;
        }
        else if ( some_number > 3 ){
            printf( "Your guess is too high! \n" );
            guess_result = 0;
        }
        else {
            printf( "Your guess is too low! \n" );
            guess_result = 0;
        }
    }
    printf( "Thank you for playing. Press Enter to exit this program." );
    getchar();
    return 0;
}
```

While Loop

In this example, the while loop function was used. The while loop allows the program to execute the code block inside it as long as the condition is met or the argument in it returns TRUE. It is one of the simplest loop function in C. In the example, the condition that the while loop requires is that the guess_result variable should be equal to 0.

As you can see, in order to make sure that the while loop will start, the value of the guess_result variable was set to 0.

If you have not noticed it yet, you can actually nest code blocks within code blocks. In this case, the code block of the if and else statements were inside the code block of the while statement.

Anyway, every time the code reaches the end of the while statement and the guess_result variable is set to 0, it will repeat itself. And to make sure that the program or user experience getting stuck into an infinite loop, a safety measure was included.

In the example, the only way to escape the loop is to guess the magic number. If the if statement within the while code block was satisfied, its code block will run. In that code block, a line of code sets the variable guess_result's value to 1. This effectively prevent the while loop from running once more since the guess_result's value is not 0 anymore, which makes the statement return a FALSE.

Once that happens, the code block of the while loop and the code blocks inside it will be ignored. It will skip to the last printf line, which will display the end program message 'Thank you for playing. Press Enter to exit this program'.

For Loop

The for loop is one of the most handy looping function in C. And its main use is to perform repetitive commands on a set number of times. Below is an example of its use:

```
#include <stdio.h>

int main()

{

        int some_number;

        int x;

        int y;


        printf( “Welcome to Guess the Magic Number program. \n” );

        printf( “Guess the magic number to win. \n” );

        printf( “You have only three chance of guessing. \n” );

        printf( “If you do not get the correct answer after guessing three times. \n”
        );

        printf( “This program will be terminated. \n” );


        for (x = 0; x < 3; x++) {

                y = 3 – x;

                printf( “The number of guesses that you have left is: %d”, y );

                printf( "\nGuess the magic number: " );

                scanf( “%d”, &some_number );

                if ( some_number == 3 ) {

                        printf( "You guessed the right number! \n" );

                        x = 4;

                }

                else if ( some_number > 3 ){
```

```
                printf( "Your guess is too high! \n " );
            }
            else {
                printf( "Your guess is too low! \n " );
            }
        }
        printf( "Press the Enter button to close this program. \n" );
        getchar();
        getchar();
        return 0;
}
```

The for statement's argument section or part requires three things. First, the initial value of the variable that will be used. In this case, the example declared that x = 0. Second, the condition. In the example, the for loop will run until x has a value lower than 3. Third, the variable update line. Every time the for loop loops, the variable update will be executed. In this case, the variable update that will be triggered is x++.

Increment and Decrement Operators

By the way, x++ is a variable assignment line. The x is the variable and the ++ is an increment operator. The function of an increment operator is to add 1 to the variable where it was placed. In this case, every time the program reads x++, the program will add 1 to the variable x. If x has a value of 10, the increment operator will change variable x's value to 11.

On the other hand, you can also use the decrement operator instead of the increment operator. The decrement operator is done by place -- next to a variable. Unlike the increment operator, the decrement subtracts 1 to its operand.

Just like the while loop, the for loop will run as long as its condition returns TRUE. However, the for loop has a built in safety measure and variable declaration. You do not need to declare the value needed for its condition outside the statement. And the safety measure to prevent infinite loop is the variable update. However, it does not mean that it will be automatically immune to infinite loops. Poor programming can lead to it. For example:

```
for (x = 1; x > 1; x++) {

        /* Insert Code Block Here */

}
```

In this example, the for loop will enter into an infinite loop unless a proper means of escape from the loop is coded inside its code block.

The structure of the for loop example is almost the same with while loop. The only difference is that the program is set to loop for only three times. In this case, it only allows the user to guess three times or until the value of variable x does not reach 3 or higher.

Every time the user guesses wrong, the value of x is incremented, which puts the loop closer in ending. However, in case the user guesses right, the code block of the if statement assigns a value higher than 3 to variable x in order to escape the loop and end the program.

Conclusion

Thank you again for purchasing this book!

I hope this book was able to help you to learn the basics of C programming. The next step is to learn the other looping methods, pointers, arrays, strings, command line arguments, recursion, and binary trees.

Finally, if you enjoyed this book, please take the time to share your thoughts and post a review on Amazon. We do our best to reach out to readers and provide the best value we can. Your positive review will help us achieve that. It'd be greatly appreciated!
Thank you and good luck!

Book 2
MYSQL Programming Professional Made Easy

BY SAM KEY

Expert MYSQL Programming Language Success in a Day for any Computer User!

Programming #10: C Programming Success in a Day & MYSQL Programming Professional Made Easy

Table Of Contents

Introduction

I want to thank you and congratulate you for purchasing the book, "MYSQL Programming Professional Made Easy: Expert MYSQL Programming Language Success in a Day for any Computer User!".

This book contains proven steps and strategies on how to manage MySQL databases.

The book will teach you the fundamentals of SQL and how to apply it on MySQL. It will cover the basic operations such as creating and deleting tables and databases. Also, it will tell you how to insert, update, and delete records in MySQL. In the last part of the book, you will be taught on how to connect to your MySQL server and send queries to your database using PHP.

Thankfully, by this time, this subject is probably a piece of cake for you since you might already have experienced coding in JavaScript and PHP, which are prerequisites to learning MySQL.

However, it does not mean that you will have a difficult time learning MySQL if you do not have any idea on those two scripting languages. In this book, you will learn about SQL, which works a bit different from programming languages.

Being knowledgeable alone with SQL can give you a solid idea on how MySQL and other RDBMS work. Anyway, thanks again for purchasing this book, I hope you enjoy it!

Chapter 1: Introduction to MySQL

This book will assume that you are already knowledgeable about PHP. It will focus on database application on the web. The examples here will use PHP as the main language to use to access a MySQL database. Also, this will be focused on Windows operating system users.

As of now, MySQL is the most popular database system by PHP programmers. Also, it is the most popular database system on the web. A few of the websites that use MySQL to store their data are Facebook, Wikipedia, and Twitter.

Commonly, MySQL databases are ran on web servers. Because of that, you need to use a server side scripting language to use it.

A few of the good points of MySQL against other database systems are it is scalable (it is good to use in small or large scale applications), fast, easy to use, and reliable. Also, if you are already familiar with SQL, you will not have any problems in manipulating MySQL databases.

Preparation

In the first part of this book, you will learn SQL or Standard Query Language. If you have a database program, such as Microsoft Access, installed in your computer, you can use it to practice and apply the statements you will learn.

In case you do not, you have two options. Your first option is to get a hosting account package that includes MySQL and PHP. If you do not want to spend tens of dollars for a paid web hosting account, you can opt for a free one. However, be informed that most of them will impose limitations or add annoyances, such as ads, in your account. Also, some of them have restrictions that will result to your account being banned once you break one of them.

Your second option is to get XAMMP, a web server solution that includes Apache, MySQL, and PHP. It will turn your computer into a local web server. And with it, you can play around with your MySQL database and the PHP codes you want to experiment with. Also, it comes with phpMyAdmin. A tool that will be discussed later in this book.

Chapter 2: Database and SQL

What is a database? A database is an application or a file wherein you can store data. It is used and included in almost all types of computer programs. A database is usually present in the background whether the program is a game, a word processor, or a website.

A database can be a storage location for a player's progress and setting on a game. It can be a storage location for dictionaries and preferences in word processors. And it can be a storage location for user accounts and page content in websites.

There are different types and forms of databases. A spreadsheet can be considered a database. Even a list of items in a text file can be considered one, too. However, unlike the database that most people know or familiar with, those kinds of databases are ideal for small applications.

RDBMS

The type of database that is commonly used for bigger applications is RDBMS or relational database management system. MySQL is an RDBMS. Other RDBMS that you might have heard about are Oracle database, Microsoft Access, and SQL Server.

Inside an RDBMS, there are tables that are composed of rows, columns, and indexes. Those tables are like spreadsheets. Each cell in a table holds a piece of data. Below is an example table:

id	***username***	***password***	***email***	***firstname***	***lastname***
1	***Johnnyxxx***	***123abc***	jjxxx@gmail.com	***Johnny***	***Stew***
2	***cutiepatutie***	***qwertyuiop***	cuteme@yahoo.com	***Sara***	***Britch***
3	***mastermiller***	***theGear12***	mgshades@gmail.com	***Master***	***Miller***
4	***j_sasaki***	***H9fmaNCa***	j_sasaki@gmail.com	***Johnny***	***Sasaki***

Note: this same table will be used as the main reference of all the examples in this book. Also, developers usually encrypt their passwords in their databases. They are not encrypted for the sake of an example.

In the table, which the book will refer to as the account table under the sample database, there are six columns (or fields) and they are id, username, password, email, firstname, and lastname. As of now, there are only four rows. Rows can be also called entries or records. Take note that the first row is not part of the count. They are just there to represent the name of the columns as headers.

An RDBMS table can contain one or more tables.

Compared to other types of databases, RDBMS are easier to use and manage because it comes with a standardized set of method when it comes to accessing and manipulating data. And that is SQL or Standard Query Language.

SQL

Before you start learning MySQL, you must familiarize yourself with SQL or Standard Query Language first. SQL is a language used to manipulate and access relational database management systems. It is not that complicated compared to learning programming languages.

Few of the things you can do with databases using SQL are:

- Get, add, update, and delete data from databases
- Create, modify, and delete databases
- Modify access permissions in databases

Most database programs use SQL as the standard method of accessing databases, but expect that some of them have a bit of variations. Some statements have different names or keywords while some have different methods to do things. Nevertheless, most of the usual operations are the same for most of them.

A few of the RDBMS that you can access using SQL - with little alterations - are MySQL, SQL Server, and Microsoft Access.

Chapter 3: SQL Syntax

SQL is like a programming language. It has its own set of keywords and syntax rules. Using SQL is like talking to the database. With SQL, you can pass on commands to the database in order for it to present and manipulate the data it contains for you. And you can do that by passing queries and statements to it.

SQL is commonly used interactively in databases. As soon as you send a query or statement, the database will process it immediately. You can perform some programming in SQL, too. However, it is much easier to leave the programming part to other programming languages. In the case of MySQL, it is typical that most of the programming is done with PHP, which is the most preferred language to use with it.

SQL's syntax is simple. Below is an example:

```
SELECT username FROM account
```

In the example, the query is commanding the database to get all the data under the username column from the account table. The database will reply with a recordset or a collection of records.

In MySQL, databases will also return the number of rows it fetched and the duration that it took to fetch the result.

Case Sensitivity

As you can see, the SQL query is straightforward and easy to understand. Also, take note that unlike PHP, MySQL is not case sensitive. Even if you change the keyword SELECT's case to select, it will still work. For example:

```
seLeCT username from account
```

However, as a standard practice, it is best that you type keywords on uppercase and values in lowercase.

Line Termination

In case that you will perform or send consecutive queries or a multiline query, you need to place a semicolon at the end of each statement to separate them. By the way, MySQL does not consider a line to be a statement when it sees a new line character – meaning, you can place other parts of your queries on multiple lines. For example:

```
SELECT
username
FROM
account;
```

New lines are treated like a typical whitespace (spaces and tabs) character. And the only accepted line terminator is a semicolon. In some cases, semicolons are not needed to terminate a line.

Chapter 4: SQL Keywords and Statements

When you memorize the SQL keywords, you can say that you are already know SQL or MySQL. Truth be told, you will be mostly using only a few SQL keywords for typical database management. And almost half of the queries you will be making will be SELECT queries since retrieving data is always the most used operation in databases. Before you learn that, you must know how to create a database first.

CREATE DATABASE

Creating a database is simple. Follow the syntax below:

```
CREATE DATABASE <name of database>;
```

To create the sample database where the account table is located, this is all you need to type:

```
CREATE DATABASE sample;
```

Easy, right? However, an empty database is a useless database. You cannot enter any data to it yet since you do not have tables yet.

CREATE TABLE

Creating a table requires a bit of planning. Before you create a table, you must already know the columns you want to include in it. Also, you need to know the size, type, and other attributes of the pieces of data that you will insert on your columns. Once you do, follow the syntax below:

```
CREATE TABLE <name of table>
(
<name of column 1> <data type(size)> <attributes>,
<name of column 2> <data type(size)> <attributes>,
<name of column 3> <data type(size)> <attributes>
);
```

By the way, you cannot just create a table out of nowhere. To make sure that the table you will create will be inside a database, you must be connected to one. Connection to databases will be discussed in the later part of this book. As of now, imagine that you are now connected to the sample database that was just created in the previous section.
To create the sample account table, you need to do this:

```
CREATE TABLE account
(
id int(6) PRIMARY KEY UNSIGNED AUTO_INCREMENT PRIMARY KEY,
username varchar(16),
```

```
password varchar(16),
email varchar(32),
firstname var(16),
lastname var(16),
);
```

The example above commands the database to create a table named account. Inside the parentheses, the columns that will be created inside the account table are specified. They are separated with a comma. The first column that was created was the id column.
According to the example, the database needs to create the id column (id). It specified that the type of data that it will contain would be integers with six characters (int(6)). Also, it specified some optional attributes. It said that the id column will be the PRIMARY KEY of the table and its values will AUTO_INCREMENT – these will be discussed later. Also, it specified that the integers or data under it will be UNSIGNED, which means that only positive integers will be accepted.

MySQL Data Types

As mentioned before, databases or RDBMS accept multiple types of data. To make databases clean, it is required that you state the data type that you will input in your table's columns. Aside from that, an RDBMS also needs to know the size of the data that you will enter since it will need to allocate the space it needs to store the data you will put in it. Providing precise information about the size of your data will make your database run optimally.
Below are some of the data types that you will and can store in a MySQL database:

- INT(size) – integer data type. Numbers without fractional components or decimal places. A column with an INT data type can accept any number between -2147483648 to 2147483648. In case that you specified that it will be UNSIGNED, the column will accept any number between 0 to 4294967295. You can specify the number of digits with INT. The maximum is 11 digits – it will include the negative sign (-).

- FLOAT(size, decimal) – float data type. Numbers with fractional components or decimal places. It cannot be UNSIGNED. You can specify the number of digits it can handle and the number of decimal places it will store. If you did not specify the size and number of decimals, MySQL will set it to 10 digits and 2 decimal places (the decimal places is included in the count of the digits). Float can have the maximum of 24 digits.

- TIME – time will be stored and formatted as HH:MM:SS.
- DATE – date will be stored and formatted as YYYY-MM-DD. It will not accept any date before year 1,000. And it will not accept date that exceeds 31 days and 12 months.
- DATETIME – combination of DATE and TIME formatted as YYYY-MM-DD HH:MM:SS.
- TIMESTAMP – formatted differently from DATETIME. Its format is YYYYMMDDHHMMSS. It can only store date and time between 19700101000000 and 20371231235959 (not accurate).
- CHAR(size) – stores strings with fixed size. It can have a size of 1 to 255 characters. It uses static memory allocation, which makes it perform faster than VARCHAR. It performs faster because the database will just multiply its way to reach the location of the data you want instead of searching every byte to find the data that you need. To make the data fixed length, it is padded with spaces after the last character.
- VARCHAR(size) – stores strings with variable length size. It can have a size of 1 to 255 characters. It uses dynamic memory allocation, which is slower than static. However, when using VARCHAR, it is mandatory to specify the data's size.
- BLOB –store BLOBs (Binary Large Objects). Data is stored as byte strings instead of character strings (in contrast to TEXT). This makes it possible to store images, documents, or other files in the database.
- TEXT – store text with a length of 65535 characters or less.
- ENUM(x, y, z) – with this, you can specify the values that can be only stored.

INT, BLOB, and TEXT data types can be set smaller or bigger. For example, you can use TINYINT instead of INT to store smaller data.

TINYINT can only hold values ranging from -128 to 127 compared to INT that holds values ranging from -2147483648 to 2147483647.
The size of the data type ranges from TINY, SMALL, MEDIUM, NORMAL, and BIG.

- TINYINT, SMALLINT, MEDIUMINT, INT, and BIGINT
- TINYBLOB, SMALLBLOB, MEDIUMBLOB, BLOB, and BIGBLOB
- TINYTEXT, SMALLTEXT, MEDIUMTEXT, TEXT, and BIGTEXT

You already know how to create databases and tables. Now, you need to learn how to insert values inside those tables.

INSERT INTO and VALUES

There are two ways to insert values in your database. Below is the syntax for the first method:

INSERT INTO <name of table>
VALUES (<value 1>, <value 2>, <value 3>);

The same result be done by:

INSERT INTO <name of table>
(<column 1>, <column 2>, <column 3>)
VALUES (<value 1>, <value 2>, <value 3>);

Take note that the first method will assign values according to the arrangement of your columns in the tables. In case you do not want to enter a data to one of the columns in your table, you will be forced to enter an empty value.
On the other hand, if you want full control of the INSERT operation, it will be much better to indicate the name of the corresponding columns that will be given data. Take note that the database will assign the values you will write with respect of the arrangement of the columns in your query.
For example, if you want to insert data in the example account table, you need to do this:

INSERT INTO account
(username, password, email, firstname, lastname)
VALUES
("Johnnyxxx", "123abc", "jjxxx@gmail.com, "Johnny", "Stew");

The statement will INSERT one entry to the database. You might have noticed that the example did not include a value for the ID field. You do not need to do that since the ID field has the AUTO_INCREMENT attribute. The database will be the one to generate a value to it.

SELECT and FROM

To check if the entry you sent was saved to the database, you can use SELECT. As mentioned before, the SELECT statement will retrieve all the data that you want from the database. Its syntax is:

```
SELECT <column 1> FROM <name of table>;
```

If you use this in the example account table and you want to get all the usernames in it, you can do it by:

```
SELECT username FROM account;
```

In case that you want to multiple records from two or more fields, you can do that by specifying another column. For example:

```
SELECT username, email FROM account;
```

WHERE

Unfortunately, using SELECT alone will provide you with tons of data. And you do not want that all the time. To filter out the results you want or to specify the data you want to receive, you can use the WHERE clause. For example:

```
SELECT <column 1> FROM <name of table>
WHERE <column> <operator> <value>;
```

If ever you need to get the username of all the people who have Johnny as their first name in the account table, you do that by:

```
SELECT username FROM account
WHERE firstname = "Johnny";
```

In the query above, the database will search all the records in the username column that has the value Johnny on the firstname column. The query will return Johnnyxxx and j_sasaki.

LIMIT

What if you only need a specific number of records to be returned? You can use the LIMIT clause for that. For example:

```
SELECT <column 1> FROM <name of table>
LIMIT <number>;
```

If you only want one record from the email column to be returned when you use SELECT on the account table, you can do it by:

```
SELECT email FROM account
LIMIT 1;
```

You can the LIMIT clause together with the WHERE clause for you to have a more defined search. For example:
SELECT username FROM account
WHERE firstname = "Johnny"
LIMIT 1;

Instead of returning two usernames that have Johnny in the firstname field, it will only return one.

UPDATE and SET

What if you made a mistake and you want to append an entry on your table? Well, you can use UPDATE for that. For example:
UPDATE <name of table>
SET <column 1>=<value 1>, <column 1>=<value 1>, <column 1>=<value 1>
WHERE <column> <operator> <value>;

In the example account table, if you want to change the name of all the people named Master to a different one, you can do that by:
UPDATE account
SET firstname="David"
WHERE firstname="Master";

Take note, you can perform an UPDATE without the WHERE clause. However, doing so will make the database think that you want to UPDATE all the records in the table. Remember that it is a bit complex to ROLLBACK changes in MySQL, so be careful.

DELETE

If you do not to remove an entire row, you can use DELETE. However, if you just want to delete or remove one piece of data in a column, it is better to use UPDATE and place a blank value instead. To perform a DELETE, follow this syntax:
DELETE FROM <name of table>
WHERE <column> <operator> <value>;

If you want to delete the first row in the account table, do this:
DELETE FROM account
WHERE id = 1;

Just like with the UPDATE statement, make sure that you use the WHERE clause when using DELETE. If not, all the rows in your table will disappear.

TRUNCATE TABLE

If you just want to remove all the data inside your table and keep all the settings that you have made to it you need to use TRUNCATE TABLE. This is the syntax for it:
TRUNCATE TABLE <name of table>;

If you want to do that to the account table, do this by entering:
TRUNCATE TABLE account;

DROP TABLE and DROP DATABASE

Finally, if you want to remove a table or database, you can use DROP. Below are examples on how to DROP the account table and sample database.
DROP TABLE account;
DROP DATABASE sample;

Chapter 5: MySQL and PHP

You already know how to manage a MySQL server to the most basic level. Now, it is time to use all those statements and use PHP to communicate with the MySQL server.

To interact or access a MySQL database, you need to send SQL queries to it. There are multiple ways you can do that. But if you want to do it in the web or your website, you will need to use a server side scripting language. And the best one to use is PHP.

In PHP, you can communicate to a MySQL server by using PDO (PHP Data Objects), MySQL extension, or MySQLi extension. Compared to MySQLi extension, PDO is a better choice when communicating with a MySQL database. However, in this book, only MySQLi extension will be discussed since it is less complex and easier to use.

Connecting to a MySQL database:

Before you can do or say anything to a MySQL server or a database, you will need to connect to it first. To do that, follow this example:

```
<?php
$dbservername = "localhost";
$dbusername = "YourDataBaseUserName";
$dbpassword = "YourPassword12345";

// Create a new connection object
$dbconnection = new mysqli($dbservername, $ dbusername, $ dbpassword);

// Check if connection was successful
if ($dbconnection->connect_error) {
    die("Connection failed/error: " . $dbconnection->connect_error);
}
echo "Connected successfully to database";
?>
```

In this example, you are using PHP's MySQLi to connect to your database. If you are going to test the code in the server that you installed in your computer, use localhost for your database's server name.

By the way, to prevent hackers on any random internet surfers to edit or access your databases, your MySQL server will require you to set a username and password. Every time you connect to it, you will need to include it to the parameters of the mysqli object.

In the example, you have created an object under the mysqli class. All the information that the server will send to you will be accessible in this object.

The third block of code is used to check if your connection request encountered any trouble. As you can see, the if statement is checking whether the connect_error property of the object $dbconnection contains a value. If it does, the code will be terminated and return an error message.

On the other hand, if the connect_error is null, the code will proceed and echo a message that will tell the user that the connection was successful.

Closing a connection

To close a mysqli object's connection, just invoke its close() method. For example:

```
$dbconnection->close();
```

Creating a new MySQL Database

```
<?php
$dbservername = "localhost";
$dbusername = "YourDataBaseUserName";
$dbpassword = "YourPassword12345";

// Create a new connection object
$dbconnection = new mysqli($dbservername, $ dbusername, $ dbpassword);

// Check if connection was successful
if ($dbconnection->connect_error) {
    die("Connection failed/error: " . $dbconnection->connect_error);
}

// Creating a Database
$dbSQL = "CREATE DATABASE YourDatabaseName";
if ($dbconnection->query($dbSQL) === TRUE) {
        echo "YourDatabaseName was created.";
}
else {
        echo "An error was encountered while creating your database: "
. $dbconnection->error;
}
$dbconnection->close();
?>
```

Before you request a database to be created, you must connect to your MySQL server first. Once you establish a connection, you will need to tell your server to create a database by sending an SQL query. The $dbSQL variable was created to hold the query string that you will send. You do not need to do this, but creating a variable for your queries is good practice since it will make your code more readable. If you did not create a variable holder for your SQL, you can still create a database by:

$dbconnection->query("CREATE DATABASE YourDatabaseName")

The if statement was used to both execute the query method of $dbconnection and to check if your server will be able to do it. If it does, it will return a value of TRUE. The if statement will inform you that you were able to create your database.

On the other hand, if it returns false or an error instead, the example code will return a message together with the error.

Once the database was created, the connection was closed.

Interacting with a Database

Once you create a database, you can now send SQL queries and do some operations in it. Before you do that, you need to connect to the server and then specify the name of the database, which you want to interact with, in the parameters of the mysqli class when creating a mysqli object. For example:

```
<?php
$dbservername = "localhost";
$dbusername = "YourDataBaseUserName";
$dbpassword = "YourPassword12345";
$dbname = "sample"

// Create a new connection object
$dbconnection = new mysqli($dbservername, $ dbusername, $ dbpassword, $sample);

// Check if connection was successful
if ($dbconnection->connect_error) {
   die("Connection failed/error: " . $dbconnection->connect_error);
}
echo "Connected successfully to database";
?>
```

phpMyAdmin

In case you do not want to rely on code to create and manage your databases, you can use the phpMyAdmin tool. Instead of relying on

sending SQL queries, you will be given a user interface that is easier to use and reduces the chances of error since you do not need to type SQL and create typos. Think of it as Microsoft Access with a different interface.
The tool will also allow you to enter SQL if you want to and it will provide you with the SQL queries that it has used to perform the requests you make. Due to that, this tool will help you get more familiar with SQL. And the best thing about it is that it is free.
On the other hand, you can use phpMyAdmin to check the changes you made to the database while you are studying MySQL. If you do that, you will be able to debug faster since you do not need to redisplay or create a code for checking the contents of your database using PHP.

Conclusion

Thank you again for purchasing this book!
I hope this book was able to help you to master the fundamentals of MySQL programming.
The next step is to learn more about:

- Advanced SQL Statements and Clauses
- Attributes
- The MySQLi Class
- PHP Data Object
- Security Measures in MySQL
- Importing and Exporting MySQL Databases
- Different Applications of MySQL

Those topics will advance your MySQL programming skills. Well, even with the things you have learned here, you will already be capable of doing great things. With the knowledge you have, you can already create an online chat application, social network site, and online games!
That is no exaggeration. If you do not believe that, well, check out the sample codes that experts share on the web. You will be surprised how simple their codes are.
Finally, if you enjoyed this book, please take the time to share your thoughts and post a review on Amazon. We do our best to reach out to readers and provide the best value we can. Your positive review will help us achieve that. It'd be greatly appreciated!
Thank you and good luck!

Check Out My Other Books

Below you'll find some of my other popular books that are popular on Amazon and Kindle as well. Simply click on the links below to check them out. Alternatively, you can visit my author page on Amazon to see other work done by me.

Click here to check out Android Programming in a Day on Amazon.

Click here to check out Python Programming in a Day on Amazon.

Click here to check out C Programming Success in a Day on Amazon.

Click here to check out C Programming Professional Made Easy on Amazon.

Click here to check out JavaScript Programming Made Easy on Amazon

Click here to check out PHP Programming Professional Made Easy on Amazon.

Click here to check out C ++ Programming Success in a Day on Amazon

Click here to check out Windows 8 Tips for Beginners on Amazon.

Click here to check out HTML Professional Programming Made Easy on Amazon

Click here to check out CSS Programming Professional Made Easy on Amazon.

If the links do not work, for whatever reason, you can simply search for these titles on the Amazon website to find them.